INTERPRETIVE WORK

INTERPRETIVE WORK

poems

Elizabeth Bradfield

ARKTOI BOOKS | Los Angeles, California

Interpretive Work

Copyright © 2008 by Elizabeth Bradfield

Book design by Mark E. Cull

ISBN : 978-0-9800407-1-5 | ISBN 9788-0-9890361-8-4 (library binding)
Library of Congress Catalog Card Number: 2007939759

Arktoi Books is an imprint of Red Hen Press
First Edition
Second Printing

ACKNOWLEDGEMENTS

The following poems appeared, sometimes in earlier versions, in the journals listed below. Many thanks to the editors for their support and encouragement:

The Alaska Quarterly Review: "The Oarfish," "Site-Specific Adaptations"; *Bloom:* "Creation Myth: Periosteum and Self," "Netting"; *Calyx:* "Endurance"; *Cream City Review:* "Concerning the Proper Term for a Whale Exhaling"; *Die Cast Garden:* "Butch Poem 2: Monstified"; *Evergreen Chronicles:* "Collecting"; *Green Mountains Review:* "Fireflies First Seen at Age 30"; *Gulf Coast:* "Wednesday Night, 9:30 pm at the Convenience Store"; *Ice-Floe: International Poetry of the Far North:* "Flooded Forest," "Whalefall"; *Isotope:* "Notes to Self on Comfort"; *Janus Head:* "After All"; *Knockout:* "Emplacement"; *Meridian:* "Butch in a Red Dress," "Now You See Me"; *No Tell Motel:* "Eight Years," "On Expertise"; *Panhandler:* "Again," "*Brachyramphus marmoratus,*" "Industry," "Love Song of the Transgeneticist," "Mid-Trip, Mid-Season," "No More Nature," "Nonnative Invasive," "Psyjunaetur," "Splitters & Joiners," "Succession," "The Voice of the Manatee"; *Poetry Northwest:* "The Shepherd of Tourists on a $20 Sunset Cruise Speaks"; *Poetry Daily:* "Industry"; *Prairie Schooner:* "Cul-de-sac Linguistics"; *The Seattle Review:* "Specimen"; *Verse Daily:* "Now You See Me".

Thanks, too, to the anthologies *Best New Poets 2006* (Meridian Press, 2006) for including "Cul-de-sac Linguistics" and *Joyful Noise: An Anthology of American Spiritual Poetry* (Autumn House Press, 2007) for including "Butch Poem 6: A Countertenor Sings Handel's *Messiah.*"

Thank you to Eloise Klein Healy, editor of Arktoi Books, for founding this press and seeing the blank spaces on the map.

A fellowship at the Vermont Studio Center and a scholarship at the Bread Loaf Writer's Conference enriched the poems of this book.

There are many people I am grateful to, many friendships that have influenced how I see and think. Let me thank in particular Linda Bierds, Jonathan Bower, Christine Byl, Stacie Cassarino, Amy Crawford, Douglas Culhane, Sara Dietzman, Jonathan Fink, Amy Groshek, Rebecca King, Scott Landry, Amy Mandel, Linda McCarriston, Mark Temelko, Katina Rodis, Raina Stefani, Gabriel Travis, Sarah Van Sanden, and GC Waldrep. My family—parents, grandmother, and sisters—deserve special thanks for their incredible support. Finally, Lisa, you are in every part of this book, inextricable; you aided and abetted and, most importantly of all, reminded me to look up from the page.

for Lisa

Contents

. . . [awaken] the mind's attention from the lethargy of custom, and [direct] it to the loveliness and wonders of the world before us: an inexhaustible treasure, but for which, in consequence of the film of familiarity and selfish solicitude we have eyes, yet see not . . .

—Samuel Taylor Coleridge, *Biographia Literaria*

Creation Myth: Periosteum and Self

Hormonally imbalanced females of all deer species
have been known to grow antlers.
This is what I choose. Periosteum rampant on my brow
and testosterone to activate it at the pedicle.
"Luxury organs," so called because they aren't
necessary for survival.
I choose the possibility buried in the furrow
which has ceased to disappear between my eyes
in sleep, in skin my lover has touched her lips to.
Females produce young each year. Males produce antlers.
Forget the in-vitro, expensive catheter of sperm
slipped past the cervix, the long implications
of progeny. I am more suited to other sciences, other growth.
Researchers have snipped bits of periosteum
from pedicles, grafted them onto other parts
of a buck's body, and grown antlers.
I'll graft it to my clavicle. My cheekbone.
Ankle. Coccyx. Breast. At last visible,
the antler will grow. Fork and tine. Push and splay.
Researchers have tricked deer into growing and casting
as many as four sets of antlers in one calendar year.
It won't wait for what's appropriate, but starts
in the subway, in the john, talking to a friend about her sorrows,
interviewing for a job. My smooth desk, my notebook,
my special pen with particular ink, my Bach playing
through the wall of another room—not the location
of the prepared field, but what the light says, when
the light says *now.*
Deer literally rob their body skeletons to grow
antlers they'll abandon a few months later.
It could care less about the inconvenience forking

from my knee, the difficulty of dressing, embracing, or
piloting a car. It doesn't care
   Essentially bucks and bulls are slaves to their antlers.
if I'm supposed to be paying bills or taking the dog
for her evening walk. There is no sense to it, no logic, just thrust.

It does its work. It does its splendid, difficult, ridiculous work and then,
making room for its next, more varied rising,

gorgeous and done, it falls away.

I

Fireflies First Seen at Age Thirty

They were in my childhood woods but dark,
dark fireflies they're called, I now discover,

quick but not chemical, quick but not light,
and so a bit of romance I find

stolen from me. When I did first
see them, it was as if I were faint

and not the evening itself dizzy
and specked with bright confusion, light

inconstant through leafed-out blueberries,
against peeling birch. Too old now

to trap with Mason jar or net and not hear
history and literature whisper across

my senses, guide my sweated palm. I held
my breath, hoped I'd stay conscious and not startle them out,

searching for a response unlayered, genuine,
true to what was there, gone, there in the woods.

Nonnative Invasive

Lupine, gentian, chocolate lily. We've been
naming, been exclaiming, been looking up
in our guidebooks the alpine flowers. *But
look at these!* Amy says, pointing
to bright dandelions at trail edge, heads

like airplane aisle lights. *How pretty! Don't you
want to pick bunches and bunches and bring them
home?* A swell of roadside by my house
yellows with them now, excessive petals
turning to excessive seed. Curbside,

I'm glad they are not lawn. But they'll invade
this meadow, push out with brash cheer
forget-me-not and wooly lousewort. I want
to reconcile them, but I can't. I hiked up
to see anemones and saxifrage, to get away

from landscaping and what landscaping
weeds out. I think of how they arrived, seeds
embedded in boot-dirt, stuck to our socks and the fur
of our dogs. *Praise their tenacity*, says Amy.
But she's just arguing a point. None of us

is glad they've hitched a ride up here.
None of us knows how to accept
the way love changes what it's drawn to
—smudging self across what's seen—
when what thrilled us first was difference.

The Shepherd of Tourists on a $20 Sunset Cruise Speaks

For the third time today, twelve miles out and back
to the whales, my voice through the PA flat as last night's
tonic. Through my patter of ecology and evolution,
I'm thinking *What can I say that will matter beyond this,*
your annual ten paid days? Then the twin engines downroar
to slow ahead, terns chirr the air, and a geyser of breath rises
as if on cue. "Just ahead at one o'clock," I say from the bridge,
"a logging humpback." The railings crowd. Cameras rise.
Empathy and longing fog the air, thick as diesel exhaust.
I can smell the long dive on the breath of the whale, fishy
and pungent. To the tide of awe, I say, "Whales
don't sleep like us. They rest one half of their brains at a time."

Then the whale dives, flukes glinting. Ashore,
the first seatings are done with their salads, barbacks
have filled sinks with ice, the town is primping its diversions
for the taffy-scented night. After the decks are scrubbed
and the candy racks stocked, I, too, will disembark,
not really thinking of whales, but full of what I've almost lost:
my own predictable and deep contentment
in their brief time at surface, the shine of thick nares
pulling open, falling closed. And as I bicycle home,
swerving around couples, squeezing between side mirrors
and telephone poles, my ears ring with breath.

Specimen

The jars themselves
were lovely. Fluted top and rounded
stopper, a few drops of condensation
pearled above the fill line.

How little we would see were it not
for context, or, more specifically, things
out of context. Flowers in a vase,
bears in a zoo, bottled fish
in a museum. The fish

inside, recurved on themselves, tails hooked
along the wall. Surreal and gorgeous—

as fluids and dyes had made
the skin and muscled flesh translucent,
the bones blue, the cartilage lines
of spine and jaw magenta.

The eye was ghostly, the gills
just a shadow of white, and
the ribs reached, their grasping
so obvious. And the tail

pulling the body to its closure.
The fins' thin stays, like the bones
of a fan. The blue kernel
of otolith floating behind the eye, waiting
to vibrate with sound.

And the whole thing
swollen by the glass that held it.
You've never seen the body so clearly articulated,
so clearly pressed against its confines.
Have I wanted enough from this world?

Succession

In the neighborhood called Magnolia
they've planted magnolia trees
to right an old mistake
made when George Vancouver's crew
saw thick-leaved madronas
on bluffs over Elliott Bay
and misnamed them. Magnolia trees
outside the coffee shop,
magnolia trees—

                              native to this continent
but not its northwest coast, land of cedar
and salal. They are leafed-out,
staked-up witness to our desire
for truthmaking—

                              outside
the post office on Magnolia,
magnolias. Magnolias glossy
and tended by the antique store, fenced
in the sidewalk by the bus stop.

Meanwhile, the madronas,
whose peeling trunks, burnt-orange and sleek,
colors layering from granny smith to pomegranate,
papery with curls I've peeled and scrawled,
here since the last glaciation,
slow-growing and picky,

                              waste away
in neighborhood parks while
beautification committees worry,
worry and try, unable to hear what for madronas
is truth: what the tree wants is burning. To burn

among huckleberry and Oregon grape
then bud from the leftover roots. Moldered
by lawn and dogs and all we've brought
with us to make things nice,
                              the madronas wait
for lightning, for some untended spark
to argue their need against our clipped
and tended ideas of care.

The Voice of the Manatee

The voice of the manatee is shrill,
harsh as a rusted pennywhistle.
This only increases my pity, my
sad head shaking at the propeller cutwork

lathed across its muddy hide because
although its screeches rise
toward the whine of machines, it can't
hear the Evinrude, all cavitation and churn

speeding the bungalow-lined and dredged
canals of Cocoa Beach. It doesn't flinch
at kids, loud with riffs of jibe and cheer,
tossing Snackables into the mangrove roots.

The pitch of harm has been recalibrated,
and the manatee's ear isn't tuned. To it,
danger sounds like distant rumble:
a car door slams two blocks away and the manatee

lazing by the culvert, suckling
the sweet water of a garden hose
left running, twitches its bulk
and slowly begins to flee.

Above, another space shuttle
flares toward space. Below,
turtlegrass grows through old tires.
Warm water flows from the power plant.

Here is what it senses: the grass is sweet,
the canal's currents slow.
A ways off, another manatee skrills:
sweet grass, still waters, warmth.

Brachyramphus marmoratus

At inlet mouths and confluences, they bob
around the boat, common enough to overlook.
If after days sailing among them I asked you
to sound their call, you'd be unable in good company.
And they don't help much, ducking
under or hustling into loft, fast-stroked
and determined, just when you've got the focus clear.

Little mottled divers. No tufts or ostentatious
bills, no plumes or bright gape—unhelpful
in snagging our wonder, which catches
on the obvious dramas
like fog on the peaks of Baranof
or chum bottlenecked at the falls.

At my desk, I whistle their simple cry,
but, out of context, its haunt is hard to conjure up.
Marbled murrelet, rare now in most waters,
nest site undiscovered until after I was born,
let me not assume that what surrounds me
is common. Let me trust that mystery still eddies,
that what's daily and familiar is worth a second look.

Pilgrimage Midsummer

Beautiful, in fog, to find and lose
the trail, the view, blueberries
low against rock. Road sound
for a while out of mind. We'd driven

hours to get here, pitched our tent
alongside others come for reasons
that couldn't be too different. But
we thought we'd lost them all,

congratulated ourselves for rising
early, choosing a trail marked *difficult*
and then going by topo-map
and gut alone. So it's no surprise

that when we scrambled up the back slope
of the park's highest peak and met
the rest of America, who'd driven up
a road we didn't know was there, hate

made us hungry. We slouched
through the parking lot to the snack bar,
tore open a bag of salt and vinegar chips,
chewed and glowered. What made us think

this view, this day was somehow stolen from us?
Kids were jumping rock to rock, popsicles
sticky down their wrists, laughing. We took a picture
leaving all that out. We walked back down.

Triangulation

I.

Quick on the bow wave's push, they rise
(though *rise* is not the right word for that thrust)
and we lean over the gunwale, lower our faces
to quick breaths shearing the water, position our gaze
so when one rolls, offering an eye, we meet it. Joy. Even
with all I know of apnea and thermoregulation,
of range and distribution, my shove of joy muscles up.

II.

Thirteen, gangly. Well-read in longing.
I've lost the Polaroid they gave me after I leaned
over the tank at Sea World and Shamu touched my cheek.
His huge, pale tongue poking through conical teeth. Black form rising
from the wrong-blue water, the water
breaking twice: in rise, in fall. I offer
this as formative. Don't tell the biologists
I know. I'd not undo that memory (small tank, his
cunning bent to its shape) first tongue, first kiss.

III.

In the wild, bottlenose are oversexed thugs.
Jerking each other off, raping upstart males
or females that trespass on their fluid turf. And yes,
I've heard the stories of pregnant women
sounded by their clicks and borne to shore,
autistic kids swum into speech through touch and whistle.
But there's also the boy whose parents paid

to let him swim among them. He flutter-
kicked and grinned, and then a male fed up
with the dog and pony show of his corralled life
took the boy down.

                         Predator, cavorter, fierce occupant
of a world designed to drown. You are not known,
after all, through any comforting thrum.

Multi-Use Area

Would the day on the hay flats—
sun slight through clouds, grasses
just starting again from last year's
grasses, geese and cranes bugling
over the marsh—have been better
without the old tires, the gutted couch
in a pullout, a moose slumped alongside,
meat taken but the head still attached?

I can close my eyes to the pop bottles,
booze bottles, and orange skeet shells
in the parking lot, along the river. Walk
past them. I can pretend my own steps
through the marsh convey a different
presence. But I can't close my ears.
There, a white-fronted goose, there
a pintail, willow branches cracking

underfoot, F-14s from the base. And there, again,
the shotgun blast and whoop which I can't
edit out, which I probably shouldn't.
It stops when I walk into view. I stop
and stare across the flats through my
binoculars, thinking *asshole*. And of course
someone's staring back at me
over a truck bed, thinking *asshole*.

II

Site-Specific Adaptations
—November, 2004

This winter, I became a man.
It happened the first week of November
while my girlfriend guided
photo tours of polar bears.

For a week in Manitoba, she wakes,
eats, and rides the tundra buggies
with tourists over eskers, lending
story to what they see. This year, though,

another landscape competes
with what's running the boreal
treeline: she and I
are on the ballot. Our home.

Our tax burden and hospital
visitation rights in eleven
states. She's wary. Bans talk
of the election. But still,

to some of them she looks
suspect: short-haired, short-nailed,
with a walk that's wide and expects
to be made way for. Out on the tundra,

she tries to keep them focused—
*Look at the fox digging
for his cache of meat.* But,
no bears in sight, a bored wife turns

from the view saying, 'So,
have you left anyone at home?'
My lover says, *A gyrfalcon!*
Until the last few years, we knew

almost nothing of their nesting habits.
It's November 2. Four more days
with this group, seven with the next,
then she'll come home to me.

What weather they're having—
mid-twenties and clear, bears
at the bay's edge in golden light
testing the new ice, hungry for seal.

Four more days in the buggy. Four more
dinners of careful talk. *My husband
is a poet*, she finally says. For the first time
not risking this truth and hating

that what she loves
could bring her to this lie.

Maid of Honor

Aqua rustle of taffeta over flattop, foreign
zipper up her spine, all up her spine,
from coccyx to nape, her un-
willowy arms in puffed sleeves,
and her mother's voice muffled but
clear: *For me, then. Wear it for me.*
It's your sister's wedding.

There's a photograph I have of her at nine
in Florida, standing by the mechanical elephant
at Pedro's mini-golf, quarter in her pocket for the ride,
one eye squint-shut, one hand in the hip-cocked
pocket of her jeans. Tomboy in a blazer
that her mother must have chosen
with her, bought for her, approved back then.

May of 1968. Palm trees flagging over astro-turf.
Yes, I think, each time I look at it, *how could anyone*
miss what she was becoming? And yes, she should
be able to straddle that elephant, sit in the red saddle
as her parents smile and wave and the upraised
trunk blows luck all over her.

She pulls up to the church on a Nighthawk,
the only vehicle she owns, swings her leg
to the ground, underskirts rustling down
over black boots. And now it's clear

to her mother on the church steps
holding the bouquet for her other daughter. It's clear
that even pumps and hose, a manicure, a waxing and,
for god's sake, some makeup, even the desire
that brought her here to *Try, for me*
couldn't make her that kind
of ordinary.

Butch Poem 1: Butch in a Red Dress

All wrong, the satin flowers
rising from the satin cloth,
the intricate frogs clasping
from her throat to just above
her right breast, her arms
from the smooth piping
of the cap sleeves.
                Especially
her arms. Not their shape, but their swing
from her shoulders, which are
held open, pushed back
to almost a parody of openness.
                  The cloth across her chest,
unprotected by pocket
or the vertical of buttons. The close pull
of dress around her belly, creased
at the bend of her, no belt
to redefine her hips.

It wasn't that her hair
was wrong. Short, yes, but
not necessarily barbered. She walked steadily
in the black high heels.
                Heartbreaking
to see her knees. Oh God, the thin tendons
at the back of her knee
connecting thigh to calf, the naked stretch
of her Achilles heel. The round, wet glitter

of rhinestone clip-ons at her lobes.
                            And I knew
I'd seen her before, drenched cat, wasp caught
behind a pane of glass, bird hunched
on a branch in a squall. I'm white-knuckled, sure
that wind will knock her from this perch—and then
she opens her mouth. And then, she's singing.

Butch Poem 2: Monstified

The summer of Dykezilla
officially began when Janice
found the rubber velociraptor
mask and pulled it over her head:

Dykezilla at the beach in swim trunks
and an inner tube. Dykezilla sniffing
cantaloupe, sitting in the dentist's chair,
at the drive-through teller's window
in her convertible, ordering takeout,
on a park bench scattering seed. Dykezilla
with the dog's head in her toothy
harmless mouth.

We have the stills on the wall. They're
fading, aged by sun, but light still winks
in Dykezilla's sunglasses
perched on her scaly rostrum—
pinup girl, superhero here to save us,
to show us what to laugh at,
and who gets to laugh.

Butch Poem 3: Considering the Femme as Trojan Horse

Look at her mingling with the PTA, chatting up
neighbors at the mailbox, handing out Halloween

candy, asking Reuben to borrow his rake. Look
at her unremarkable stride, her unremarkable hair,

her easy expectation of welcome. Look at how they
smile and wave as they pull out of their driveways.

They can't go back now. She's already known to their dogs,
to their kids, and when she strolls to the annual picnic, to which

she's been invited, she carries with the rhubarb pie
a love of girls like me.

Butch Poem 4: Losing a Father

With him, something left her, some hook
by which she gaffed the world
and held it to sense, to love, to logic

despite the awkward ground she'd learned
to claim. His best son, at his side
she cleared gutters of leaves, shoveled

the drive, changed the Chevy's oil,
sat back after dinner
heavy in a chair. She learned

to be a gentleman. Hard at first for him
to see her tapping out his cigarettes,
wearing his old belt and shoes, to see

what she took as her own.
He came again to love her,
and to love even what rested silent

between them. And she knew her luck.
But when he died some of her swagger,
some of her bullheaded sureness, some hope

to be praised for the likeness she'd made
was shaken. I have no metaphors to lend this,
just witness to her decentering, just certainty

that only the loss of her mother
—the self she made herself against—
could be more difficult.

Prodigal

I always loved the prodigal son's story, returned ratty
and thirsty, embraced having recognized
the sweet water of home's well. But
his story is not mine. Aside from one thing,

this love, I was the good daughter: schoolwork,
babysitting, home before curfew. Now I see
it is our families, not we, who are returning
from turning away. Where

did they go? To the sneer of neighbors,
the clucking of tongues. To the straight
and married place they'd hoped
we'd end up, and they waited.

We never came. So they've come
to find where they left us. Holidays,
your mother pulls you aside
to criticize your hair, your shoes, your

short nails. But later, when it's dark
and the neighbors can't tell who
is working in the garage, though of course
they know, she says she's glad you have my love.

And my grandmother, on her eightieth birthday,
wanted portraits of the families that her daughters
had made. She told the photographer, in front
of everyone, to not forget us, you and me,

paired in the spot where my married cousins
had posed with their children. So there we are,
on her wall, spotlit, shocked, and grinning.

Infrared Reflectoscopy

I.

You can't guarantee this sanctioned tom-peeping
does nothing. It may not be harmless to expose

the artist's reconsiderations. Perhaps just a skew
to the pigment, perhaps a wedge in the time-crack

of drying oil that later fractures cheek, fruit,
the sky's thin veneer of blue glossing what had once

been seraphim. Or do the rays excite a shadowed self?
Maybe the hound by the boot of the lord, brushed

into shadow, is now shaking off his inferiority
complex, readying to return.

II.

I ask my grandmother if she thinks her silent
husband, gone twenty years now, would have loved

what I've become. I know he'd rather not be shown
what has forced up through the girl who followed him,

learning to hook worms, row, split wood
and shape cigar smoke into rings with her tongue,

who I feel underneath these layers of time I wear,
who I recognize in my cast shadow. I know that to him

she was considered complete,
and this reworked self not intended.

Concerning the Dog

The dog is depressed. Note
her lackluster wag,
her excessive midday naps.

The dog is lonely. She's found it
difficult to make friends
and strangers seem

frightened she may bite,
which hurts her feelings.
Me? I'm fine. But the dog

is clearly having difficulty adjusting,
is misunderstood. The dog
needs a better bed, needs

a vacation, a rewarding job,
a wave from the neighbors.
Look how she bows,

gentling herself before
children and grandmothers.
Look at how they, given

chance, despite the pit bull
of her head, allow themselves
to love her.

In Which I Imagine I'm Not the Only One

She's been feigning boredom
to sneak off from her parents and her younger sister
unfollowed, her toe wet from the mouths
of anemones and horse clams she's been pushing into
just to see them jet their improbable hold

of receded tide. Once she reaches the old house
down the beach—the cabin,
really, of a ship beached in a storm, hull deep
in the channel but the pilot house tossed to shore—
she ducks into the metallic

cool and her breath, echoing, is joined.
And what happens there? Fumbling
under the rusted roof where barnacles
purse their lips. Flood tide

between their legs. Tanned clavicles
gleaming in the dim light, straps slipping from them.
Eyeliner pulled onto fingertips, blurred
across breasts.

By the time I become her niece
and am old enough to walk that far,
the cabin roof is gone to salt, the sides
tilting to sand, only a suggestion of themselves, but
still recognizable. And inside on that August day

back when the house was still whole, they weren't
pretending or practicing. They were swollen
as books left to dew, pages too thick
to close. You can see it, can't you,

in the family photos where I
am the only one coupled to my own
sex. Look closely. She's glancing at me, at us,
over the heads of her married children,
past the beard of her husband, my favorite uncle.
She's remembering. I want her
to be remembering.

III

Emplacement
—May, 2004

Nine months in Boston, four years
on the Cape not enough, I
have missed it: this year
the cicadas rise from the ground
which was not their grave,
husks buried and breathing.
I have returned west. Alaska,
this time, no reptiles to speak of.
Here, to my east, the Chugach
make the horizon, huge and unchanging.
Mosquitoes rise from the bog
as they do every year. How I miss
the turtles, box and painted and
the prehistoric snappers
of Clapp's Pond. I miss, too,
spring peepers and crickets and
I don't know how to miss
the cicadas, which I've only read of,
their odd-yeared resurrection, their
sudden winged and six-legged flood.
And what else rises with their song returning
and my leavetaking? It is the year
when in Massachusetts men
are for the first time marrying men,
women marrying women. I call back
to hear how many cakes L has baked
and bowers T's woven. People here
say I'm from the East Coast.
Because I last lived there. But
it's untrue. I have never seen those bugs

crawl out and begin their intolerable
or amazing rasping. What wild and excessive
celebrations I have missed.

The Science of Reconstruction

Turn a wheel and the velociraptor
stripes pink, dots chartreuse, swirls mustard—
choose one, the sign says, *all*
are possible.

᷍

          I imagine, given
the known variables, how you miss me
when you're out in mangroves, eskers,
or fjords showing people
what to see in what they see,
how I'd like you to miss me:
                      A bird flushes
and my gasp startles in your chest. Your mouth
wets at a scent in the air that associates.

᷍

The astronomer shows stars
gauzed by rock concert fog,
backlit and pulsed. He shows
solar winds pluming around novae, noble
gasses in coronas. Slide after slide
we gape.
            Then he tells us
he's made what we're gawking at
through filter and algorithm, picked colors
for the elements, designed, in effect,
our awe. Without his help,
he says, we'd think
nothing was there.

Wednesday Night, 9:30 pm at the Convenience Store

Not a girl, really, tall
and close to stooping—the checkout
girl's nametag reads "Winsome."

Which I don't think she is.
Stoic, maybe. A little fierce
under the red glow of the Marlborough
display panel. Enduring
the poly-blend polo where I read her name.

Her mother couldn't have been winsome
at that moment of naming. Sweaty. Sore.
Stitched a little at her crook, words
grunted out.

There's another woman in town named Flowers.
I worked with her in the kitchen. And another
named Quince. Are they real,
these names? Hello, my name
is Flighty. My name is Bitter.
My name is Crass. Yearning. Shellacked.

Hello, Winsome, handing out
lottery tickets, slightly disapproving, although
expressions's hard to read across
your flat cheekbones, your flared nose.

And thank you, Winsome, for bagging
my convenient half and half, my loaf of bread.

Winsome, thank you for
my dollar seventy six in change.
Thank you, Winsome. Winsome, which neither
of us could be. Winsome,
thank you for the slow woman ahead of me in line
deciding between credit or debit. For what
you offer. For whatever made me look up
from my scattered, selfish life and read your name.

Mid-Trip Mid-Season

Cocktail hour in the lounge & today
the special is "glacial flowers"—muddy
booze, blue ice. I am not allowed
to drink but must mingle, chat, smile.

I pretend that I smoke. On the crew-only
fantail: diesel fume and drone,
the slow wear of my hearing. But
breeze. But sea. But permission

to be silent and expectant. In the lounge,
they're comparing colleges and home towns,
that other kind of history. No one wants to know
what's outside unless it's off the charts—a bear

swimming to a moose being ripped
by killer whales while a wolf pack howls
on shore, bald eagle glaring from a cedar snag.
That kind of thing. Otherwise they're exhausted

by attending, by my demands to *look,*
look—to look at the broad blur of vista,
no points of interest assigned by placards,
and find wonder. Whether we see anything

on the brochure or not. And I
am not yet tired of looking but
have lost for a while the will
to ask the simple questions

that open a place to being seen: *Where
are you from? What made you come
to Alaska? What did you hope to see?*

Industry

She paid my dad a nickel
for every crow or jay
he brought her. Not
easy money, scattering
from the old oak at any sound.

He learned to line a few
into one shot, carried them home
like trout, legs tied to a string,
feathers glistening marine, arm held up
above the field's wet grass.

Her foot, trundling
the sewing machine, counted
out his pace. The feathers
caught every light, and she would look
down as she pushed them

into needle, into cloth, into
hats and ties she hoped to sell,
her thoughts punctuated by the spit
of his gun, the hoarse protest
moving to a further tree. Sometimes

she thought she felt the feathers lurch
beneath her hand, but this was difficult
to confirm, or even to mention aloud.
Superstition, the ruffle of down
in a closed room, does not bear

that weight. Only the feathers
restless with color in a basket.
Only the machine's hum
whispering to her: *fly*.

Splitters & Joiners

All the sparrows and their mottlings, the adaptable
gulls breeding across category, how do we tell
them apart? Or the new-world tyrants—willow
and alder flycatchers—so alike that only song
separates them? We separate them.

The old arguments beat against air, scientists
on either side: splitters and joiners. Which
best serves truth, that there are more kinds
or that the two are close enough
to call *species*, call *same?*
                              This morning,
in Maine, the dove tells me *All so*
sad   sad   sad
                        calling in this place
among places I can't call home having left
too quickly. Having left even while joined, discovering

        Vashon   Duwamish   Stellwagen   Chugach

Allow me to be responsible to you, to see
how you are linked even if unearned by years
or birth. Allow me to consider which (*separate   same)*
will best serve this patch of cranberry, salal,
this stand of shore pine, madrona.

Rock dove, pigeon, linked in field guides but
what difference between rooftop and wild field.
Blue grouse split this year to *dusky* and *sooty*
because we noticed something new. They are
joined to us. Separate from. These birds

with their own stories and associations, flying through the groupings we imagine and impose. Not unaffected, though, by the long, strange echoes of their names.

Notes to Self on Comfort

birch balm
bog balm
balm of sphagnum and reeds
dune balm (sand collecting in all cuffs and folds)
sea balm at the sounding edge balm beyond the shore's smudge
balm of a mackerel sky overhead, vaulting
grass balm and the first mower loud across it—spring
thunder balm
balm of a black bear wide-legged on dwarf dogwood balm
of my thrilled fear
nuthatch at the feeder—balm of birds arriving
leaf balm (shadow dapple on afternoon walls)
balm of bees at the flower box on the balcony above the five-lane balm
of berries picked in sun
kelp balm
barnacle balm
balm of white-winged scoters rafted in a cove, muttering then
scattering out across the flood tide and over
        oar balm, bow balm, keel balm rowing
pond balm (lilies fooling the dog who thinks they're earth and jumps
from the dock
snorts and gallops back to shore)
thicket balm and grove balm
blossoms balming down from a tree in the sidewalk
dawn noon dusk night and what stars filter through, the balm-glint
is it enough to ease what's lost? go further
past what's easy   past what's passing
and find the balm of the small things all around you
the balm of the small

Love Song of the Transgeneticist

Transgenics: the science of transferring genetic material
from one organism into the DNA of another.

Like chimes, these tens of vials
in their shallow tray as I take them
from the room of electronic arms to
the room of electronic eyes. Like
the cut drops of a chandelier
trembling at footfall.

                     Because it's late, because
the chief technician's home—
sighing over the heads
of his children lined up before the tv, which they love
with the pure desire of an equation: evening = blue
light on the far wall + someone prompting laughter
$\div$ a father's unamusement^n—

                         because I'm here
alone and love the cool glass
warming in my palm
               I select one.

        In the lab, beneath
the long, audible bulbs, a fan turns on. New note
in the underlying hum of machines at wait. Like
monks chanting, this sound; like the buzz
I heard once by a river, the earth's own
stasis, its churning; like the overlapping breaths
of animals in a barn midwinter.
                I bend
my imperfect retina to the machine that allows magnification.

    This is what we've done: frozen
      golden orb and common garden, ground them

to brown powder. From that
the single gene extracted, injected, birthed.
Raised the goat through its bleating, its
stubborn first year. Then pulled the warm pink teats,
smelled the white froth, skimmed the fat,
salted the skim and watched the foreign protein curdle
and sink like snow. Separated the powder
into vials. Added water,
spun the thick, gold liquid into strands.

My mother disapproves. Silk from a goat?
(click of knitting needles) You must
(purl two) know what
you're doing (dropped stitch), dear.

This is what we will provide: medical sutures
that will dissolve, no need to recrack
the body to retrieve them; fishing gear that, lost, will not
catch and drown, catch and drown in its own tide,
unhauled; lingerie to stop the bullet
that would kill a prince, a cop, a nurse
on the front lines; and more unimagined.

In the electron hum, in the stoppered vial
a dust—like vapor becoming rain. Look. We've expanded
the world's possibilities which, I know, I know, were
already more varied than our catalogues
and abstracts reveal.
                    Look at the white sift
illuminated, its perfect, tensile form.
Another machine breathes
to life on a timer someone's set.

This is what we promise: It's safe. You
can drink it. The chief technician
took some home and poured it on his children's
cereal (wheat-free, as they've developed this allergy;
their cupboards careful, also, of strawberries, of corn,
the borrowed things in husks and cells).

O, our shifting fractal views of what is beautiful—
aqueduct, thresher, cesarean, quark, heart valve,
Tupperware, pygmy goat, microchip, cul-de-sac—
this silk woven from a loose helix we all share, these
small fingers of glass, my script naming each one,
the notebook heavy in my lab coat pocket.

  When I step outside
   (airlock, airlock, punch code, guard)
into the sweet, fluid night,
my favorite sound: Little bells
on the red-collared goats
in the compound's pasture.
         Still
possible, still in the process
of becoming.
     And I whisper to them: It will
be better. It will be of help. It will
answer our undeniable need.

Remnant

Wedged between the floorboards, for back then factories
still had floors that creaked and splintered, that gave, that shone
with knot and grain when swept at a dim-lit workday's end.
Tumbled in the air vents. Not just the stray sequins themselves,

scattered cosmos of glamour, but the small round punches
of metal made to give them hold, the bright filings smoothed
from cut edges. Years later,

as he built dividing walls,
installed plumbing, and made a home
beneath the ductwork in this space
still unheated Sundays, he gathered them.

At first, glittering piles studded with lint at his broom's pull. Then pink discs
shaken from his hair, plucked from his cheek in the morning, falling
into the saucepan from the old pipes and narrow ledges

above his broom's reach, marking random pages of his books. Exhaled in sneeze.
In truth, he liked them winking from the lintel's seam. He liked to think
his home was built from the raw stuff of metamorphosis—
girls to princesses, broad-lunged women to divas, slight men
to pretty dancing things—

Where now are the hands
that punched the small discs out,
that tinted the sounding sheets of metal, that filed
the sharp edges smooth? The women, bent to the bright sift
of their labor, grew heavier with each breath.

They lie now somewhere quiet and in their own
ritual finery, all dust
but for where their lungs rest—
glittering wings. Furled.

Sweater for a Giant Squid

after a sculpture by Mary Carlson

And now I see how bare the body is, how fleshy,
all underbelly and membrane, all slick
and interior. Pull its tentacles
into the long, long sleeves. Hood
its large eyes. Clothe it. Make it

decent. Hide us from the shocking bareness
of its eight bare arms.

There are a few other things that could stand to be clothed—

raccoons splayed along the roadside, chicken breasts
in cellophane, my fear that love will leave me, new buds swelling
from the maple

that dream I had last night, ripped
through the warm cardigan of dark.

IV

Cul-de-sac Linguistics

Today, the boys call each other penis.
Hey penis, commere, penis, pass me the ball,
penis. Last week it was *whore*, discovered

halfway through a game of h o r s e
on the mini-hoop that backs my fence.
And earlier this afternoon, the teenage girls

whose bedroom window stares
above my thumbnail yard improvised
outgoing messages in theatrical rapture:

first the easy scatological, then
a nursery rhyme that morphs
into an anti-homo riff so suddenly

I actually look up

to see if they're directing this at me
(they must be), down in the yard, reading poetry
as my girlfriend weeds the flower bed.

O, the high profanity of kickball games,
the rough posturing demanded
by even this tame street. Listen, they're learning

how well bastard fits with fucking, how ass
can't be mis-used. No one could hope to ease
their jagged entries into this profane world

which is fucking beautiful, ass-bastard gorgeous,
the evening light wild and soaring
like kickballs on a true arc into flowerbeds

of penis tulips and pussy daffodils
that nod their heads in wild agreement
with the whorish, shit-loving lot of it.

Endurance

There's a woman now
swimming the English channel
or the Bering Sea or across some other impossible water
between unimportant shores. Miles
of it. She sips from cups
extended over the waves on a pole.
She cannot hear voices
and measures time in breaths.

I'd love to see her entering
the water, capped and suited, greased
for the psychological edge of speed and warmth and
to save her skin from the pickling brine. I'd love
to see her stumbling out on the other shore,
knees unused to weight, buckling.

Of course this is how
I see love—something of endurance
and unreasonable calm.
Harder to attempt once you've known
the numbing tiredness, the unrelenting salt,
the safe boat unable to gather you up
if you want the miles to count for anything.
And you wade in anyway.

Remodeling

—for Lisa

We want a hole in the north wall, a hole
then a window, for light, for the green spruce
just beyond the vinyl siding. We've managed
to forget the night last spring

when Emilio, Michael, and Pierce, whose baseballs
we return, who we lecture on the sensitivity
of tomato plants to hockey pucks, who ring our doorbell
selling chocolate and wrapping paper

    . . . we've almost forgotten the night last spring
when the boys climbed the shed roof
and saw this:
         my shirt up around my neck,
your hand on my breast, my body beneath
yours, moving.

When I opened my eyes and said *shit*, you
buried your face in the couch, as if
they might assume your short hair meant *man*,
as if that might be better. And instead of cursing

them, instead of throwing open the window
and telling them off, I pulled the blinds and hid.

And for months we skulked to the mailbox,
walked the dog in distant parks, imagined
the stories rumoring and how they'd sound
when they reached the parents:

They were doing it in the back yard, under spotlights,
charging admission. We didn't admit

to each other that we waited for the spray paint,
the busted taillights. Worse, we were ready
to understand ... But now

we want a window in the north wall.
We want the spruce-shade. We want
to announce how much we love
the sky, how its light finds us, too,
even here.

Now You See Me

The neighbor whose daughter last week
sold me thin mints and caramel delights
asks *Where's your friend? I haven't
seen her around lately.* Before
I answer: Are we (is she) speaking

code? When I answer, friend
will mean lover. When I say partner,
I mean lover. Girlfriend means lover. A date
is a fruit that is full of sunlight, thick
with sweetness. I want

to ripen in full sun. Let me
put on my magic cloak, take it off.
Now you see me. On the airplane
the stewardess can't quite put

her finger on it: *Sisters? Cousins?*
She comes back with an extra bag of snacks.
*There's something . . . have I met you
before?* No. No. And yes—

At the credit union: Elizabeth, Lisa
on the joint account. On the title
to the house. Catalogues
and address labels come unsolicited
with an amalgam of our names. But

we don't kiss at the front door. Don't shout *sweetheart*
down the street. Don't flaunt and so can't
resent it when we're invisible here. Neighbor,

if you put on the glasses provided
with this poem, the neon
over our garage will be hard to miss. Now
you see us. And there are others,
houses all around you lighting up.

Butch Poem 5: Recognition and Praise

Blinking in the turnpike restroom
when Jenny walks into the Ladies,
the matrons and bachelorettes
of New Jersey recognize a butch.

The grocery store clerks, too,
of Alaska or Florida, saying *sir*
when Lisa buys tampons, not looking close
or maybe looking closer than the rest.

When I spot them on the street, in line
at the movies, unmistakable, here
is what happens: love floods me.

Butch Poem 6: A Countertenor Sings Handel's *Messiah*

Seven verses in, he has stepped out from the tuxed
and taffetaed quartet of soloists. He has begun to sing:
Behold, a virgin shall conceive, and bear a son, and shall call
his son Emmanuel. Amplified by good acoustics, the hall
is rustling accompaniment to the countertenor's solo:

Lift up thy voice with strength; lift it up, be not afraid.
Arise, shine; for thy light is come. From my seat
next to my parents, high in the mezzanine,

I can see heads turning, bending toward each other,
toward the program, small lights coming on
above the paper. My parents restrain
themselves. But the rest of the hall
is turning to the biography. Is lifting
opera glasses. Is straining ears to hear him:

Then shall the eyes of the blind be opened,
and the ears of the deaf unstopped. He is singing
the alto's part in her key, his voice light and clear.

Whispering underscores the music:
    What is this high, sweet voice in a tuxedo?
I am transfixed. I want to reach under his starched
shirtfront and find a different sex. Listen to him—

He was despised and rejected of men; a man
of sorrows, and acquainted with grief.
He's singing the score and another story alongside it:

He hid not his face from shame. Through
these old words, he is making song
of the drag queen and the bulldyke.
Let him sing without the accompaniment

of rustle. Let him sing without any doubt
between body and voice: high but not shrill,
more lovely than the wide-skirted soprano,
the chunky tenor, the dapper bass. I watch
his shine-parted hair, his weight shift at key change.

*Thou art gone up on high, thou hast led captivity
captive, and received gifts for men.*

Afterwards, in the bar, where anemones
splay open and salmon flick through
canals designed for our wonder, no one
mentions the countertenor. My parents,
I think, are trying to navigate the appropriate
path of the moment, as am I. But he's all
I can think of, his rolled r's, Adam's apple
lifting his tie at crescendo. Onstage,

*Then shall be brought to pass the saying
that is written, Death is swallowed up in victory.*

billed as high culture, this unsettlement,
this beauty applauded at last.

Butch Poem 7: In the Mexican work visa office

you were invited to sit in a battered chair before a battered desk. He looked at your face, your tits, your name, Lisa, its soft vowel finish feminine in any language, and recorded your responses to surname, eyes, hair, then checked the box next to *masculina*. At least that's how I heard it when you came home and told me about the green book used to track you there and how you had been named. It turns out the page reads *masculino*, a less true label for what I love in you, a step removed from rightly describing your body, the shape of air displaced as you're walking toward me, my masculina.

A Celestial Observation

At 5:51 a.m. EDT on Aug. 27, 2003 Mars was closer to our planet than it had been in nearly 60,000 years. The next time Mars may come that close is in 2287.

Bright red pulse,
portside running light
of a vast and distant battleship
passing close enough
to raise concern. I don't

go out. I don't get up
when the alarm goes off.
Friends ask *did you see?*
and I am ashamed
to tell them the reason
for *why not?*

Who of my blood will be alive
to compare it in that distant
future? No children

of children of children
will look up and wonder
what it—red and solitary,
as yet unsloganed, as yet
unmarked by colonizing lights—
what it would have cast across this face

here, now, looking up, tired
and cranky yet still able
to marvel at time, at the long reach
of the past and the insistent pulse

of my own red blood
dammed in the reservoir
of my body.

After All

This is why I won't
have them after all, though
I love the warm curve
of their foreheads, their babble
and tangle of hands in my hair.
Though I have sought them
as teacher and false aunt, drawn
to them, the heavy parts of my body
drawn to them, let
my sisters have them, answering "none"
when asked years later what dreams
had been thrown over. Answering
none, and meaning it.
Sweetheart, I know
I have wavered and sometimes
longed, but let me say now
that even if what fluid things
passed between us
included sperm, I would not.
When I write that I want
to shake your teeth
from your skull or wonder
what else could have filled
the space you take, you know
it is my heart's downpulse
and its own incomplete truth,
a thing created to be released. But
to live with the measurable growth,
the doorjamb penciled higher
each year, the vocabulary
approaching what of this world

is difficult, comprehending, making
an individual sense—
I would want to hate her,
mock her, love her wrongly
across the page, daughter
I will not have, in poems.
And I could not bear her
to read them.

Netting

She wants so badly to catch something, net held
over a reflecting eddy. She's pulled in
jewel-eyed frogs, their toes
splayed on the canoe's smooth hull,
throats throbbing. She's captured
small snails and, once, some roe, but mostly
just bottom muck, silt, and thickening leaves. Again,

into the water lilies and duckweed, the heavy sack
of ooze deep within the net's bell, weight
unexpected as a breast's warm heft. Inside, mummichogs
and sticklebacks torque themselves and she sifts
through the black spill for shrimp. The net
bends heavy from her hand,
spills over. Reach into my chest,

into the bone sieve where I keep my heart, and this
is what you'll find. Substance black,
thick, and silken: staining the lines of your skin,
smelling potent and determined,
shot through with green ribbons of grass,
silver things twitching and gasping in it,
remarkable and ready in seconds to drown.

Concerning the Proper Term for a Whale Exhaling

Poof my mother sighs
as against the clearcut banks near Hoonah
another humpback exhales, its breath
white and backlit by sun.
                              Don't
say that, says my father, disapproving
of such casual terminology or uneasy
with the tinge of pink tulle, the flounce
poof attaches to the thing we're watching, beast
of hunt, of epic migrations.
                              But I'm the naturalist,
suggesting course and speed for approach. They
are novices, and the word is mine,
brought here from the captains I sailed for
and the glittering Cape Cod town
where we docked each night
after a day of watching whales.
                              Poof,
Todd or Lumby would gutter,
turning the helm, my cue to pick up
the microphone. Coming from those smoke-roughed cynics
who call the whales dumps, rank the tank-topped talent
on the bow, and say each time they set a breaching calf
in line with the setting sun, *What do you think of that? Now that's*
what I call pretty, then sit back,
light a cigarette—coming from them,
I loved the word.
                              And even more
because the dock we returned to each night
teemed with summer crowds, men lifting
their hands to other men, the town

flooded with poufs free to flutter, to cry, as they can't
in Newark or Pittsburgh or Macon, to let
their love rise into the clear, warm air,
to linger and glow
for a brief time visible.

V

The Oarfish

It took three people to carry its length, sagging
between their hands, from the wrackline
where they found it, down to the water's edge.
From a distance just a pale smear along the beach, probably garbage,
probably a ride of sand, driftwood, but something
in its snaked lie made them walk up
and look. And then lift it. I wasn't there,

but have stared so often at the snapshot
I'm convinced I could have been, and that's
good enough, isn't it? To look at a picture and feel the sun
on your shoulders, the dead weight
of the fish, the shifting rocks underfoot, hot
through the thin soles of canvas shoes, the smell
of insect repellent and decay.

This strange long weight that they picked up—
serpent, discovery, trophy, documentation—a thing
no one else they'll ever know
will have seen. Yes, they'll nod
to the guidebooks, it's like that, but
not quite.

The red was more subtle. The belly
not so sleek. We held it. Scales glimmered on our skin
after. I wish I had been there.

It's curled and ghostly on the wall.
They picked it up and smiled, they
sighted down the long fin of its dorsal. The two
plumes trailing from its head, flaring
like oars, rested on the inside of their upturned arms.

Collecting

Tangled in seaweed, too smooth
to walk by without touching, I pinched
the purse of it, found it whole.

Held between my eye and the sun, some
long-tailed thing flicked
beside a yolk. Whip-like,
random in its panicked life.

Crab husks, skate cases, urchin tests, the thick
and calcified rings of barnacles—I've only recently
begun collecting. What a waste,

those high school science classrooms, specimens
left out on the shelves. But then the pale, stiff flesh of them
said nothing to me.

Kitchen knife. Cereal Bowl. A washed out spice jar.

The husk cut like celery, fibrous, and fluid poured out.
A longer slice and that was all of it, veins red
against the melon of flesh and yolk,
gills feathered out like roots, fins just forming.
Still flicking in the bowl.

Shark, skate, who knows
what I stopped it from becoming when I slid it
into alcohol. Mine, this paused and stiffened life, since
I picked it up and put it
in the dark, possessive well of my pocket.

Psyjunaetur

Iceland: The Night of the Fledgling Puffins

New school shoes an excuse for boxes
to save, unflattened, in garages, in closets, under beds—

the shaded, angular nests lined with tissue
or bluff-grass, ready. The year is

closing down, the world's light moving from the long Icelandic
summer, its remnants pooling in lamps, sconces and other

humming beams that work to trick the body when dawn
comes late. Then it happens. Uncalendared but expected.

Hatched, fledged, hungry, the candy-billed young set out
to see if it's true—*In the lighter sky, where stars are doubled*

and the moon's twin shines beneath you, herring glide in flocks
thick enough to overspill a thousand beaks & you can fly

through vast & oily feasts. They ruffle and launch from rock cleft toward
what glow they see, the streetlamps, where children wait

with outstretched boxes, catching them, nesting
them, carrying their slight palanquins to the sought shore,

learning from this tenderness, years later, when the birds
return, how delicious are the things we've freed.

Flooded Forest

Silk mangrove leaves, plastic fruits, the snipped ends
of green wire tying them to vines.
She's hollowed out a maple log
to hold the aquarium pump
disguised in a back corner. She
buries grass into the gravel, adjusts the angle
of a fallen branch, creating a cross-section
of forest, a slice of the Amazon in spring.
                              There's a name
for the annual flooding. For when the water
rises up around the trees and fish
eat fallen fruit.

          We can go weeks without kissing. Veiled
          in preoccupations. Tired. Irritated
          by the very breath of each other
          sounding in a shared room.

Some leaves, lacy brown, waft
toward the bottom. The aerator percolates,
bubbles glinting toward the surface.
In a week, she'll introduce the first fish
to this strangely constant
approximation of their habitat.

               Then, for some reason or another,
          according to some clock we share, desire. Or
          one of us begins to build a place
          for lust to fin through.

It's the idea, she says, of fish swimming
into the nests of birds. Of eels coiled in burrows.
Of water transforming just by its increase.
Of what the fish do to take advantage.

Whalefall

I hadn't really thought about it, to tell you
the truth, those bodies sinking
to the ocean floor. The term

sounds like nightfall,
and I picture them coming down
like a huge and lazy rain,
like hot air balloons landing in an open field—that
silence and fascination as
anything meant to be suspended
touches earth.

It's frightening—the arrival,
the dust, the realization that this
is not graceful after all.

There must be an archipelago of whalefall
along some lines in the ocean—greys
beside California, humpbacks along
the Carolinas. Swimming
and then falling, their bones silent and then landing
and then settled.

The ocean floor is more vast
than the myth of Wyoming—endless
plains, plentiful herds, sky
uncharted still. Cattle
skulls glinting white between the grasses
picked up, decorated with turquoise, hung
on a barroom wall. Not death then, but watchfulness, memory
in its white and hollow-socketed form.

I've been trying to decide
which I love more, the dark bodies
falling or the pale and teeming scatter of bones
in the unlit sea. Or maybe it's just good to know
about landings. The awkward,
gorgeous reconciliation
with the ground.
Honestly? I need to believe
in the beauty of falling.
The stunning ache of descent and then
its unexpected practicality—
new habitat. Decorated and watching.

Again

Already, you don't know
what has passed, or when, precisely, it started.
The sky has been shifting
                              into something red
for over an hour, and you've been blinking,
taking a sip from a glass, turning
a page of your book,
daydreaming.

The moment is close. The light is condensing
into a smear of orange along the horizon,
                                      and then
something happens—bee trapped
inside the window, crash from the kitchen—
and you've missed it.

When I was small, my father once had me race up
a long flight of unsteady, wooden stairs
yelling *run* at my heels. *Go.*
Faster, or you'll miss it.

And at the top of the stairs, we
watched it again, the sunset.
                        And that changed everything.

He was thinking of math, the earth's curvature and
the great trick of altitude. He was thinking
that he'd like to see again
the sun slip into that particular evening's end.
And why shouldn't he?

Pointing off across the bay, out of breath,
he lifted me to stand on the shaky rail
where I swayed above a steep fall
of blackberries, bees humming around the fruit as if
they were in orbit around dark, clustered suns,

                                thinking the sun couldn't know
        what we'd just gotten away with.

I knew it wasn't magic, that time can't be fooled. My legs burned
from the run. I knew it was just quickness. Light.
The relative pace of things. Our willingness
to find ourselves out of breath above a humming decline
of pollen. The sunset
twice in one night, leading me
to all this longing.

Eight Years

We pulled snowshoes from the back and crossed the five-lane
by the sports bar between two bad curves,
headed to the bog. It was midday,

sky low, traffic a light drone. We cinched
straps, stomped teeth into the trailhead,
took snapshots of ourselves and set off

for the muffle of woods and the snow we hoped
now would carry us, and mostly didn't, but still
seemed somehow better as we followed

tracks, reconstructed pounce and dodge, waiting
for the place to raise voice. And when it didn't
we turned toward home, stopped listening, and I

started mugging for you, showing off, and I thought
as I ran along the trail, snow slapping up the backs
of my thighs,
>   *maybe we have found it, the thing*
where neither is better or cares or clocks the length.
The thing that makes us beautiful.
>   And when I turned
to shout back, what escaped was

Moose. Dewlap swinging, shoulder hump

rocking in gait, heading out of the trees
the way I'd come, toward you.

Somewhere, there's a tally sheet that reckons up
how often we say we're happy and mean it,
and we, in the messy and reasonable panic
of our lives, just lost our chance to earn a point.

The moose ran out from the trees and I ran back
to you and we stared and backed away together,
frightened by the huge answer of its body.

Off the Beach

For a while there were six of them
or seven. Even with binoculars and steady
attention, I can't say. But our entire purpose then,
for that span of time we weren't yet sure of,
was to watch them rise and breathe. To see
their odd skin surface and sink back through a wave.

We didn't need to say much. My
parents. My sisters. The whales
couldn't tell or didn't care
that we continued watching. But we did.

There wasn't much exclaiming. There wasn't
much drama, but, I suppose, relief
that such a simple thing, a thing
so out of our grasps, should perform
this task demanding our attention. Could allow
each of us, in our own way, to attend.

On Expertise

Adding it up, it seems I've lectured to at least six
thousand people—day upon day upon day in season—
and still I know nothing about whales. How do they
come together and then part? What does the force
of water against their rorqual pleats feel like

when they lunge up through a ball of bait? Like running full out
to the end of a leash? Like a blast in mouth
from a gas station air hose? I know
I would gladly stand again and repeat my facts
of length, weight, and anatomy. I'd pay again

the price of repetition, of showmaking
in order to find them each day, if we can,
in the bay. Then   watch   listen   smell
as shearwaters gutter in their froth.

I know nothing. But what could I ever know,
no matter the abstracts and whalers' logs.
What other than my own unscientific surge
at the Latin in my mouth, the epic chronology,

the anecdotes, the recognized flukes, the flex
of pectorals as they fall to slap the water, *Megaptera
novaengliae*—if I tasted you, if I swam your migration,
if I tuned my ear to your song, even then.

No More Nature

No more nature we say after fourteen hours on the water in August,
skin ready to crack, lips too tender to close. *No more nature*
in November when blackfish strand in the salt marsh

and we've stood in sulphur muck as the tide falls out to dark,
their breath whistling hard as we dig pits for flippers
scraped raw by sand, as vets try to predict which

could survive until flood, which should get the syringe
of chemical sleep. *No more nature* after the storm blows up
while guiding kayakers across the bay, which means towing home

the shoulder injury, prow lunging the chop, tow rope
cinching the gut. *No more nature* after waking before dawn
to band birds in first frost, shin after shin ringed

with numbered metal, wing after wing teased from nets
until we almost forget how frightened their small hearts made us
when we first held them. No more, we can't take it, can't

resuscitate our wonder, can't keep up with its unrelenting.
But then we have a beer. We take a shower. We decide
to walk around the pond and look for turtles. After all,

we could see a coyote lapping its reflection, we could find
the nest of the great horned owl that calls each night
as we lie in bed, unable to not listen, unwilling to miss anything.

NOTES ON THE POEMS

"Creation Myth:" Quotations are taken from *The Rut: The Spectacular Fall Ritual of North American Horned and Antlered Animals* by Ron Spomer (Willow Creek Press, 1996). I recommend it thoroughly.

"Fireflies First Seen at Age Thirty:" Members of the beetle family Lampyridae include the "true" fireflies as well as a member native to the Pacific Northwest that does not bioluminesce.

"*Brachyramphus marmoratus:*" Until 1974, the nesting site of marbled murrelets was only speculation. No actual nest had been seen by scientists. It turns out that these relatives of the puffin nest solitarily and far inland on branches of old-growth trees—quite strange for a marine bird. In California, Washington, and Oregon, marbled murrelet populations have declined precipitously due to habitat degradation. Southeast Alaska is the uncontested stronghold for marbled murrelets. On the water there, they are seen and heard daily.

"Infrared Reflectoscopy:" This technique of art restoration allows conservators to use infrared light to see beneath the surface layers of paint, lacquer, and varnish to whatever lies beneath.

"Splitters & Joiners," often called "splitters and lumpers" or "hair-splitters and clumpers" represent two basic philosophies of classification among biologists. The lumpers like to group variants into a single species while the splitters prefer to call each variant a different species. For example, at one point in not-too-distant history there were over one hundred named species of brown (or grizzly) bears in North America. Today there is just one, *Ursus arctos*, with several regional sub-species.

"Endurance" was inspired, in part, by the open water swimmer Lynne Cox.

"Psyjunaetur:" Like many marine birds, puffins, once they fledge, do not return to their nesting site until they reach sexual maturity, perhaps as many as four years later. Puffins and puffin eggs were (and in some places still are) sustenance for many northern peoples.

"Whalefall" is the term for whale carcasses on the sea floor. Once fallen, the whales are scavenged by detritus eaters and then colonized by bacteria and creatures that live by converting fat to hydrogen sulfide through chemosynthesis. The ecosystem of whalefall habitat bears remarkable similarities to that of deep-ocean hydrothermal vents, and many scientists believe that whalefalls serve as bridges for life between vents.

Elizabeth Bradfield grew up in the Pacific Northwest and has since called Cape Cod and Alaska home. *The Atlantic Monthly, Poetry*, and *Field* have published her poems, as well as the anthologies *Best New Poets 2006* and *Joyful Noise: An Anthology of American Spiritual Poetry*. Bradfield's awards include two Pushcart Prize nominations, a scholarship at the Bread Loaf Writer's Conference, and a Wallace Stegner Fellowship. She holds an MFA from the University of Alaska Anchorage and is founder and editor of Broadsided (www.broadsidedpress.org). When not writing, she works as a web designer and naturalist.

www.ingramcontent.com/pod-product-compliance
Lightning Source LLC
Jackson TN
JSHW081332130125
77033JS00014B/520